Greater Than a Tourist – Amsterdam, Netherlands

50 Travel Tips from a Local

> TOURIST

Julianna Smolenski

Julianna Smolenski

Copyright © 2017 CZYK Publishing

Lock Haven, PA

ISBN: 9781521298619

DEDICATION

This book is dedicated to the music makers and the dreamers of dreams, those who wander by lone sea breakers and sit by desolate streams, the world losers and world forsakers for whom the pale moon gleams. This book is for the movers and the shakers of the world in hopes that they find that they are not alone. Go.

Julianna Smolenski

BOOK DESCRIPTION

Are you excited about planning your next trip?
Do you want to try something new while traveling?
Would you like some guidance from a local?

If you answered yes to any of these questions, then this book is just for you.

Greater than a Tourist — Amsterdam, Netherlands by Julianna Smolenski
offers the inside scope on Amsterdam.
Most travel books tell you how to travel like a tourist. Although there's
nothing wrong with that, as a part of the Greater than a Tourist series this
book will give you tips and a bunch of ideas from someone who lives at
your next travel destination.

In these pages you'll discover local advice that will help you throughout
your stay. Greater than a tourist is a series of travel books written by locals.
Travel like a local. Get the inside scope. Slow down, stay in one place, take
your time, get to know the people and the culture of a place. Try some
things off the beaten path with guidance. Patronize local business and
vendors when you travel. Be willing to try something new and have the
travel experience of a lifetime.

By the time you finish this book, you will be excited to travel to your next
destination.

So grab YOUR copy today. You'll be glad you did.

Julianna Smolenski

CONTENTS

16. Get Some Good Eats

17. Walk It Out Again!

18. See an Exhibit

19. Watch an Independent Movie

20. Support the Arts

21. Enjoy Some Opera

22. See the Tulips

23. Get on Top

24. Get Happy

25. Stroll Through the Red Light District

26. Eat and Be Merry

27. Get Prepared to Stray

28. Feeling Beachy?

29. Go, Van Gough!

30. Head South for Carnival

31. Live Local

32. Visit The Hague

33. Love Your Children

34. Interact with NEMO

35. Check Out That Zoo!

36. Experience Dutch Kiddie Culture

37. Spend the Day at Slagharen

38. Dive with the Dolphins

39. Cuddle with Cats

40. Stroll Through Jordaan

41. Eat your Vegetables

42. Try Some Chocolate

43. Eat the Best Dutch Apple Pie in Town!

44. Sing-A-Long

45. Stop for a Drink

46. Grab-And-Go!

47. Unwind in Westerpark

48. Check out Westergasfabriek

49. Plan for Festival Season

50. Party Like a King

> TOURIST

Author Bio

Julianna Smolenski is a Long Island (pronounced: Lawn-guy-lind) New Yorker who lives in Utrecht, Netherlands. She enjoys long walks with nature, getting lost in the moment, laughter filled evenings rich in conversation, full bodied wines, and warm weather. Julianna has visited some 20+ different countries, 100+ cities all over the world, unendingly falling in love with the natural treasures of the world and its inhabitants.

WELCOME TO > TOURIST

WHY AM I A LOCAL?

I'm a local expat living in a changing city. Right now I live in Utrecht, which is about 30 minutes outside of Amsterdam. Amsterdam alone is swarmed with expats; students, job seekers, mail-order brides, musicians... you name it... from all over the world. The difference? I speak Dutch.

One of my first goals upon moving here two years ago was to learn Dutch. I daresay that ninety-eight percent of all Dutchies speak fluent and perfect English, but not many expats even bother to learn Dutch, especially native English speakers. But me, I'm a rare commodity. A tri-lingual native English speaker, an American at that. Unheard of. I've use this skill to integrate stealthily into Dutch culture and share these tips with you.

When I first moved here from the Big Apple, I lived in the South, near Eindhoven, the city of light. I decided to move to Utrecht almost as soon as I came here. Utrecht is where the cool people live. If Amsterdam is Manhattan, Utrecht is Brooklyn. A lot of people who work in Amsterdam live in Utrecht, leave the big city hotspots for the tourists and leave the chill vibes and lekker biertjes for the locals.

What's amazing about Amsterdam is how diverse it is. It's alive. It's beautiful. It's underground. Things are happening in Amsterdam, but you won't hear about it from a tourist website or an event planner. You hear it from the city itself and you let it find you. Everything is here.

You want to go for a walk in the park or along the canal? You can do that. Art Gallery? You betchya. Go to an underground club, you can do that too. Get some shopping done? Take your pick. Prefer to buy local? The market is open. Gluten free/Paleo/Vegan? You can eat here, too, friend.

Amsterdam is the big city, but I've never loved a city more than Utrecht; every fiber of my being resonates with it. Every day I live my dreams and every night I go to sleep and dream again.

1. Walk the Walk

The Netherlands is pretty famous for its heavy bike culture. You see the streets lined with bikes tied on poles and bridge lines, bike racks, parking garages, and bike shelters conveniently located just exactly where you need it. Bikes are used for everything here, it's an essential part of every day life.

If there's one thing that Dutch natives resent most it's tourists walking in the bike lanes. If you want to make your stay here as pleasant as possible this is the most vital rule to obey: Don't walk in the bike lanes. You can imagine the frustration of someone trying to catch their train or make it to work on time, and then a group of tourists stop in the middle of the bike lane to take a selfie. Please don't.

2. Pay Attention

For non-Dutch tourists the commotion can feel pretty extreme at first, especially if your first stop is Amsterdam. So many moving parts. Bikes, busses, trams, cars, and other miscellaneous automated vehicles, not to mention pedestrians. It's a lot to take in. The trick is to look all ways before doing anything. Left, right, in front, behind.

You have three rings of traffic, essentially. The outermost, pedestrian, lane is where you'll most likely start off. Pay attention to your surroundings. Before moving, check where the bikes are, see where other people are coming from, look for any motor traffic. Take it slow, breathe deeply, don't make any brash decisions.

As with any big city, stopping in the middle of the road causes a chain reaction and a load of resentment that you don't want to be responsible for. Feel like taking a photo? Check your surroundings and find a good spot to stop. Looking, being aware of your surrounding, and paying attention are always your best bet.

3. Obey Traffic Signals

Holland is one of the most meticulously well organized countries in the world. Things work here. Part of things working is the understanding that in order for things to go seamlessly, every cog in the machine needs to work together. As an American hailing from the Big Apple, I'm just not used to this. In New York you have things that are made to look like they work but don't actually. So we jay walk, do our own thing, else you will spend your lifetime in wait.

This is not how it works in Holland. There are weight sensors on the bike paths and auto paths that work on a timer in accordance with the pedestrian crossing signal, as well as bus and tram signals. As a pedestrian or cyclist, the button to cross will actually work when you press it. Busses and trams run on their own lines. Left and right turns are orchestrated to be more efficient with traffic influxes. Everything is put together to go one and then the other. The signals change quickly and frequently.

Every day someone who thinks their common sense is great decides to jay walk and is unexpectedly greeted by a car trying to turn left or a tram. Don't let that be you. Until you've lived here for awhile you're just not prepared to make these calls. As a tourist it's much better to be patient, enjoy the view, and watch the traffic signals.

4. Walk Before You Bike

Amsterdam is a pretty small city. You can see all of the major tourist destinations in one day by foot. Use the first day to walk up to Dam Square, Leidseplein, the Rijksmuseum, and the Red Light District. Follow the canals and see where they'll take you. Go ahead and take a canal tour. This will give you a good understanding of the city, how it works, how it feels, and grant you a bit more comfort for the future of your stay.

I made the mistake of renting bikes on the first day when my best friend was visiting. After two years perhaps I'm immune to the overwhelming sensation of biking next to twenty other bikers and all of the other passing vehicles from the street. Before I knew it my friend was lost in the crowd. She was not used to it. Lesson learned.

5. Cruise the Canals like a Local

Once you explore the city on your own and are feeling comfortable enough, rent a bike. This way you can explore the further parts of the city and have more time to really get to know them. You'll find tons of places to rent from just outside of the train station and on almost every corner while you're in the heart of the tourist district. I've had a good experience with the Holland Rent a Bike on Damrak 247. For every rental place that I know of you need a credit or debit card and are required to leave a tentative deposit of €200.00, charged only if you fail to return the bikes. You shouldn't pay more than €10/day, the average price is usually about €8.50, though you'll most likely want to rent it for multiple days to get a real feel for the city.

6. Check Out a Coffeeshop

You could argue that your trip to Amsterdam would be a waste if you didn't at least go into a coffeeshop. Keep in mind that Dutch coffeeshops, while they do serve coffee, are not famous for the tasty dark pick-me-up. Entry is 18 years and up, and a lot of places require that you buy a drink before being seated. Alcohol is not served in the coffeeshops, so you can choose your favorite non-alcoholic beverage, my favorite is pear juice. The bigger Amsterdam chain is Bulldog, sporting a restaurant/bar and of course coffeeshop. My preference is in De Pijp (see #9).

If you're new to smoking marijuana or if you don't smoke very often and aren't sure what you want, most places have a comprehensive list, much like that of a beer menu, of the type of high you get from each blend. You can buy it straight by the gram or you can buy pre-rolled joints and spliffs (tobacco and weed). Most Dutchies smoke spliffs, they even use the word "joint" to refer to a spliff, "puur" (pure) meaning that it's only MJ.

If you are, on the other hand, no stranger to MJ and friends, and are looking for something more intense, ask the people who work there. In terms of magical mushrooms, for example, they usually don't sell caps to tourists but if you are explicit that you do a lot of 'shrooms and are looking for something more they can usually set you up. Whether your a beginner or an expert, the people at the desk can be extremely helpful when you're trying to choose, they're completely used to people not knowing what they like and can easily advise you. Don't be shy to ask though. I talk about this more later, but in Holland you really need to use your words.

7. Follow the Footsteps of Anne Frank

Part of the beautiful culture of Holland is also the immense sorrow it faced during WWII. The people of Holland have not forgotten and seem to be constantly looking to the past and comparing it to the events of current. In my opinion this reflection acts as a way to keep people joyful for what they have, what is not, as well as to remind them of what "us vs. them" mentality can cause.

One of my best friends in the Netherlands is obsessed with Anne Frank, in an almost spiritual way. He took me on a tour through Amsterdam Zuid, the neighborhood in which Anne grew up before her family moved into the annex, which is known as the Anne Frank Huis (House) now. Anne Frank Huis is open to visit if you're committed enough to wait three hours in line or lucky enough to get a ticket online a few months in advanced.

There is an app called Anne's Amsterdam, which is currently unavailable to Apple users. So, if you're an Apple user like me, you'll need to find a friend with an Android phone or use your imagination for this app to work. Every house affected by WWII is marked by golden stars in the front sidewalk that state the name, lifespan, and place of death of the former inhabitants. With the app, you can trace Anne's house where she grew up, see the school she went to, book store where she bought her famous diary, ice cream parlor where she used to visit, and other cited landmarks from the diaries. There's also a photo gallery that links up places where you are with famous photos from that time in history. WARNING: These can be very sensitive. You will feel things.

8. Eat Your Feelings in De Pijp

All of that heartfelt touristing can be really draining. If you do make it to the Zuid area, you'll want to check out De Pijp. My favorite place for coffee is actually Scandinavian Embassy, it's very tiny and probably crowded but the filter coffee is a step above the rest and the food is just my taste. C&T Coffee and Coconuts, which is right around the corner, is much bigger and has a larger variety of coffee, food, juice, and other drink options. Make yourself at home, the ambiance here is very, very cozy, or as we say in Holland: gezellig. For breakfast I really like Goût Deli in Oude Pijp Markt. They have a bunch of pre-made things that you can take away with you but also there is room for sitting. Fresh jus d'orange is a must here. The Dutch are crazy about orange juice, well orange everything, really. Fresh pressed OJ and free wifi are two things that you find everywhere in Holland, even in the sketchiest of all bars.

9. Walk It Off

Had enough eating? Walk around the market square in De Pijp. Saturdays is the market, you can find tons of hand made local goodies, not to mention all of the other wonderful shops in De Pijp. Had enough of the crowds? In the area of all of these things is Sarphatipark. It's usually pretty quiet and always very beautiful. Spend a minute catching your breath, take a minute to relax. Feel like smoking a bit? Katsu is a coffeehouse in the De Pijp Markt (market square.) The prices are more reasonable than central tourist areas and the staff is really great in helping you choose the bled that you're looking for.

10. Wine And Dine

If you're in De Pijp at night time this is also a good spot for dinner. Although I personally prefer to come here for brunch, or lunch, dinner is also possible. Wijnbar Paulus is a very trendy wine bar in the area, but as far as I know they do not serve food. Luckily, de Pizzakamer is right down the road. Both of these places are always bumpin' and filled with laughter. When you're done you can catch the tram back to your hotel without a problem.

"My experience in Amsterdam is that cyclists ride where the hell they like and aim in a state of rage at all pedestrians while ringing their bell loudly, the concept of avoiding people being foreign to them."

Terry Pratchett

11. Be Direct

One of the most famous aspects of Dutch temperament is their directness. The Dutch don't side-step things or skirt around what they're trying to say. You want something? Have a question? Aren't sure? Just ask! Dutch people aren't used to being expectant of what you're thinking or trying to say. Use your words and things will unfold for you.

Dutch people can be extremely helpful and overwhelmingly kind, all you need to do is make your concerns known. They're not mind readers and don't assert what they think that you are feeling or trying to ask. If you need something and just look confused, nobody is going to ask you if you need help, they'll just go on about their business. You need to ask. This was really so difficult for me at first and often people confuse this way of being for rudeness.

The way I see it, people here are really independent and treat you as they expect you to treat them. If there's something that they need help with they will, without hesitation, ask. You don't need to assert. So naturally, out of human nature, they imagine that you would do or act the same.

12. Know the Lingo

A few basics of Dutch language will go a long way. Here are some staples:

ij = y In Dutch they use a soft J. You'll see a lot of words with **ij**, which may look bizarre if you're just not thinking in Dutch after 10 minutes of visiting. Understandable. Since so many things are spelled with **ij** it's good to know this little thing, saving you the embarrassment of asking where "De PiJp" or "RiJksmuseum" is. Think of it as "Pype" or "Ryikes Museum"

Noord en Zuid = North and South These come in handy on the train because it's just so different. Noord is pronounced phonetically. Zuid is more like Zowed (Think "Cow-ed" with a "Z")

Bedankt or **Dankjewel = Thank you** Pronounced: Be - Donkt or Donk yuh vell

Alstublieft = You're welcome Pronounced: Ahls tube leaf

Fiets = Bike Pronounced: Feets

Lekker = Literally Almost Everything The spelling is phonetic. Food is lekker. Girls are lekker. The weather can be lekker. This whole day can be lekker. Anything enjoyable can be lekker but the word itself means "yummy"

13. Ride in Style

Aside from bikes, the second most popular method of transportation in the Netherlands is public transit. Navigating the Dutch public transit system, however, could easily lead to one's undoing. The system itself is extremely well organized but it requires people to know just so much more than they are capable of knowing as a tourist. Foremost, you need to check in and out of just about everything. You can buy an anonymous transit card (OV Chipkaart) for €7 at the train station customer service desk. You can use this card for all public transportation, you just need to load it up (minimum balance to ride the train is €20) for the amount of traveling you want to do. You can, of course, buy each ticket individually either at the machine or, if you need to pay in cash, at the customer service desk. If you're riding the bus or tram you can buy it from the conductor as you board. Knowing where you're going is the second tricky bit.

14. Download These Apps

If you don't feel like buying an international data plan specifically for your trip, you can easily rely on the abundance of free wifi literally everywhere. From the moment you step off the plane: BOOM! Free Wifi. In the train? Free wifi. Cafe? Free. Shady bar? Wifi. On the bus? Yups. You're covered, don't worry.

But for those times in-between wifi spots and you've got no idea where the heck you're going, **HERE** (a.k.a. "**HERE we go**") is a good app where you can download the map of your region. Holland is a small country, so you can download the whole country, whereas in larger countries you can only do it by region. It works really well and doesn't leave much out. Google Maps also allows you to download the map of your area but my experience has been more positive with HERE.

9292 is the app used by the public transportation system in the Netherlands. You just set in your starting and ending points and the app will give you step-by-step directions on how to get there, as well as a variety of time and location options so you can get there as soon as you want. There are also functions to change the departure time or to plan for an arrival time, so you can plan for future trips.

15. Pamper Yourself

I've never heard of death by enjoying life too damn much, but that doesn't mean it couldn't happen, I suppose. Although it's not something Amsterdam is terribly famous for, it is home to quite a few relaxing spas and wellness centers.

For ladies, you can check out the Oosterse Vrouwenbadhuis, (Eastern Women's Bath House) conveniently located just outside of the lovely Westerpark. This public bath house offers a variety of spa treatments from scrub treatments, Eastern Massage, and bridal packages. General entry price is €17, towels and other bath items are available for rent or purchase.

For those who prefer a more co-ed atmosphere, Sauna Deco is not a bad option. They have a variety of different sauna and steam rooms, an outdoor sitting area, and a lounge/cafe area. There is also the added option of massage, ranging from €37-65. Entry prices vary based on date and time, on average €20 per person, excluding towel/robe rental. No swimsuits allowed. (Re: You will see things.)

16. Get Some Good Eats

Feelin' a bit fancy? Head over to the Museum Kwartier. My friend recommended me this amazing Asian Fusion place that lay therein, MOMO, which now I can recommend to you. It's very trendy, very chic. Be sure to make a reservation, this place fills up fast, especially on the weekends. Couldn't get a seat? No worries.

Across the street is Max Euweplein. There you can choose from a few different restaurants, my favorite of which being Wagamama. Less fancy but still ambiguously Asian, on one side they have their noodle bar which has a great variety of Asian cuisine, on the other side is the sushi bar where you can pick the sushi off the conveyer belt from their covered plates. Don't worry! Each piece has their expiration time on them so they're not just sitting out for hours on a conveyer belt. Chefs make everything fresh where you can see them.

17. Walk It Out Again!

Still in the Museumkwartier? Check out Wondelpark. This beautiful park goes on for days. Better to enjoy in the daytime so you can do a full loop of the extensive park. There are many cafes, ponds, fountains, doggie paths, open areas where you can find street performers, and public restrooms. Also a good place for a picnic if you're in the mood. If you begin in the Museumkwartier you can make a full loop back to the Museumkwartier or you can exit at the other end, which is Overtoom. There are some nice things to do in this area as well, such as check out the theatre, as well as quick bites and fancy sit-down restaurants, such as Adam Amsterdam. If you keep walking in that direction you'll also find Rembrandtpark, which you can choose to visit the same day or save for later.

18. See an Exhibit

Like any major city, Amsterdam is spoiled with different types of exhibits, galleries, and museums. If you're in the area of Rembrandtpark you'll maybe want to check out Shellman Art Gallery. Shellman is an interior design gallery where the art is made out of, you guessed it, shells.

MOCO (Modern Contemporary) Museum Amsterdam is a popular contemporary and modern art museum that focuses on taking "a glance into the art world which is usually hidden to the public." They tend to exhibit more hidden jewels of the contemporary art world, the crème-de-la-crème of edgy artwork.

Niewue Kerk (New Church), located in Dam Square, is one of the more significant expo centers in the city. The history behind the church-turned-gallery is as interesting as the exhibits themselves.

Stedelijk Museum is a contemporary art museum that shows international and modern art and design. Their focus is on the new and upcoming artists, often within a political context. Located in the museumplein it's in spitting distance of Van Gogh Museum and Rijksmuseum, and also has its own cafe so you can make a day of it.

K = Galerie is a little hole in the wall arts and craft design gallery not too far from Dam Square. What's unique about this place is that it's not really one thing or another, a bit random and hodgepodge, but you get a feeling of collaborative artistry here.

19. Watch an Independent Movie

As an American this was one of the cooler experiences while living in Europe. Watching independent movies in another country allows you to really get into the way of life, feel like you're apart of the life of a local, even though you're just watching it on screen. The movie I saw was in English with Dutch subtitles. Since Amsterdam is such an international city this isn't uncommon but I can't honestly say if it's always accessible to non-Dutch speakers, though I imagine so. The one that I know, De Balie, Kleine-Gartmanplantsoen 10, hosts debates, theater, an talk shows with a social or political focus. There's also a bar/cafe and you're allowed to bring your drinks into the theater. There are, however, other independent theaters throughout the city.

20. Support the Arts

Amsterdam is a hub for the lesser praised creative arts and is filled with loads of venues where you can experience all different types of art.

Het Muziekgebouw is a popular concert hall which hosts a variety of musical performances all throughout the year, even multiple different showings in a day. They also have a cafe inside with a lovely, airy ambiance that gives you a feeling of refreshment before you begin your music-listening.

De Kleine Komedie is a performance arts center focused on Comedy. They offer a variety of live performances ranging from stand-up to cabarets. Look on the website for performances available in English by selecting "Language No Problem."

Theater Bellevue is another performance arts theater that hosts drama, dance, music performances, and more in both Dutch and English. The website actually is very user friendly so you can easily find a performance that you're interested in and can understand.

"En ik heb je lief, oho

Kom zon, kom maan

Beschijn de stad met z'n bruidskleed aan

Kom sterren, kom nacht

Er wordt een nieuwe tijd verwacht

Want het gaat verder, het gaat door

En ik heb je lief, oho

Hallelujah Amsterdam"

Rameses Shaffy

"And I love you, oho

Come sun, come moon

Dress up the city with its wedding dress

Come stars, come night

A new time is coming

Because it continues, it goes on

And I love you, oho

Hallelujah Amsterdam"

21. Enjoy Some Opera

Interested in indulging in some more refined entertainment? While there are many places that you can view opera, some of which have already been mentioned, the following are some of the more well-known and consistent venues specific to Opera and its twirly sister, Ballet.

Het Nationale Opera & Ballet (The National Opera & Ballet) is the official hub for opera and ballet performances. Conveniently located in Waterlooplein, this opera house offers a variety of performances and events throughout the year, including luncheons and children workshops.

Nederlandse Reis Opera (Dutch Traveling Opera) As the name implies, much like a traveling circus, this opera is coming to a city near you. If you're interested in a bit of a more edgy-contemporary opera with fresh takes and rising talents, check their website for when they're around your area. From Amsterdam some other options are Utrecht, Rotterdam, and The Hague (Den Haag).

Following the contemporary vibe, Silbersee on the Northern side presents to you the lesser-known, unorthodox productions of musical theater and experimental opera. To give you a flavor, their upcoming lineup as I'm writing this includes true colors, cage out, and homo instrumentals.

22. See the Tulips

Happen to be visiting in the spring time? Well, all that rain is not for naught. Make your way over to Keukenhof, the floral paradise where you can get up close and personal with all of those lanes of bright colored tulips that you flew over on your way here. At Keukenhof they make interactive, well designed displays for the tulips unlike any other botanical garden I've ever been to. It really feels like you're here to see the tulips perform, their bright and vibrant beauty is really being accentuated. There are cafes and gift shops all around and, of course, a little Nijntje garden (the animated rabbit sensation of every Dutch family home.) Spend the day walking around in awe of every bright colored bulb in this beautiful garden. You could literally spend the whole day here and still not want to leave.

23. Get on Top

Especially good in the summer when it's not raining, Amsterdam is home to many lovely rooftop cafes, bars, and restaurants.

For a nice brunch, lunch, koffie verkeerd (café-au-lait), or dinner, head over to Canvas, the rooftop cafe of the Volkshotel (people's hotel.) Go straight after entering and take the elevator on the left up to the second to last floor. I prefer to come here for light snacks and cocktails, though I'm sure their dinner options are also top. From here you get a beautiful overlook of Amsterdam Zuid, so if you did do the self-made Anne Frank tour this is a nice wrapping up point. Also it's gorgeous.

Floor 17 can be found on the topof the Ramada Apollo Amsterdam Center. Their fine dining restaurant serves quality meals from organic and local ingredients between 6:00 P.M. all the way into the wee hours of 11.00 P.M. You can also come here for a spectacular breakfast, or check out their rooftop for a relaxed afternoon wind-down. For a special treat, check out their website to plan for one of their movie nights. After 10 P.M. Floor 17 opens SKYBAR. Come here for some luxury cocktails, mock-tails, wines, and bubbles. Bit sleepy after all that partying and bubble-drinking? For a pretty penny you can also sleep on top in what they call the Air-Bubble.

SkyLounge is probably the more well-known of Amsterdam's rooftop bars. Located on the top of the Hilton (your landmark to finding this is the Starbucks at the base), SkyLounge is conveniently located just a hop and a skip away from the train station. Come here for drinks after a day out, but make sure you dress top. It can get a bit pricy, but the champagne cocktails are so worth it.

24. Get Happy

If you're wondering what the LGBT nightlife is like here in the Netherlands, it should come as no surprise that it is bumping. The gay bar that my friends and I most frequent is Taboo, appropriately situated in between Amstel and Herengracht (men's canal) near Rembrandtplein. This area is known amongst locals as the "gay district." If you roam around this area enough you will find a plethora of rainbow flags and safe spaces. Also, many of them do happy hours and Drag Bingo, as well as Karaoke. We are your friends.

There are also some fetish/kink/BDSM type of clubs. For all of you fantasy needs, check out Church. They have frequent fetish parties as well as cruise nights.

Furthermore, for those who enjoy being gay and free, Amsterdam is the place to be for Gay Pride Festival. The time changes every year but it's traditionally in the summer. Bring your glitter and platform shoes, rainbow everything, just no judgement. People here really let loose, you really don't want to miss it.

25. Stroll Through the Red Light District

Whatever your stance be on prostitution may be, this area sparks a multitude of different conversation, challenging people's preconceived views of what "should" or "should not," what's "right" and what's "wrong." Many tourists find the Red Light District to be a fascinating chunk of culture, reflecting upon the values of what makes a society successful, thriving, or healthy. If you try Googling "Red Light District" you won't find it on the map. You will find "Red Light District Tours," which is a good place to start. You can also search "Oude Kerk" or "Old Church." The Red Light District is placed ironically behind the back of the Old Church as a sort of statement to the Church. If you really want to behold these lovely women you really need to comb through he streets but, please do not take their pictures. First, it's super disrespectful, second it's illegal. Many Dutch people don't enjoy the conversation surrounding prostitution, since for them it's simply a better option than rape and pimping culture seen in more restrictive societies, so better to skip on asking a local for their opinion, though I know it's tantalizing.

26. Eat and Be Merry

All over the Netherlands you can find legal squats. Abandoned buildings that people have taken upon themselves to turn into modern speak easies. I'm not honestly sure if some of these places are pure squats or if they're just regular establishments, but the gist of them is bonfires, group feedings, beer from the supermarket, and often some form of entertainment, donation based or cheap at least. My first encounter of this is RLGC44 Recycle Lounge Gallery Club in Amsterdam Noord. I don't think this is a squat per-se, but it's definitely one of the more underground clubs in Amsterdam where you can meet some cool locals who will maybe take you out and show you the real underground world of Amsterdam. Party begins around 7 P.M. for dinner, drinks, bonfires, and of course recreational drug use.

27. Get Prepared to Stray

Done with the tourist district? Check out the surrounding areas. The great thing about Holland is that it's so small, so if you've got a week or two you can see the whole country. Take a few days to check out some of the towns in the surrounding areas. Warm enough for a beach tour? Want to see more Van Gough with fewer tourists? Looking for something a bit more real? The next few chapters will explore all of these possibilities. Still got that OV Chipkaart?

28. Feeling Beachy?

When the sun is shining and the days are long it becomes difficult to resist the calls to sandy beaches and ocean waves at Zandvoort. My first time visiting the Netherlands it was late July. I had just enough jet-lag to stand down in a battle against Cthulhu but not enough jet-lag to sleep the entire day, so my friend thought, accurately, that the best idea would be to unwind at the beach.

For some reason, unbeknownst to me, every time I come to Zandvoort, no matter what the rhyme or reason, I wind up at the same spot: Skyline Beach Bar. All of these places are honestly interchangeable and food trucks scan the coastline so you're never out of reach of anything, but for one reason or another this is the one I always wind up at. It's not too far from the train station, their selection is perfectly average, the ambiance is beachy and refreshing, and the staff are adequately kind.

Spend the day parked up on the beach soaking up the sun and then come in for some lunch, snacks, or cocktails. You can even request a boozy smoothie if you're at a conflict of choice. Cure your sweet tooth with a Dame Blanche (hot fudge sundae) or their tiramisu mousse. Or you can opt to pick some cookies and ice cream up from the food truck. Dare to dream, my friends!

29. Go, Van Gough!

Outside of Van Gough Museum in Amsterdam, the second largest collection of Van Gough paintings can be found at the National Park de Hoge Veluwe in Gelderland's Kröller Müller Museum. Around the museum you'll find an outdoor auditorium, a sculpture garden, Van Gough Café, not to mention access to the rest of the national park. Each section of the park is a perfectly manicured landscape so lovely that it becomes unsure whether the landscapes are the inspiration for beautiful art or they're maintained in inspiration of beautiful art. Either way, your mind is sure to explode. The whole park is made accessible by white bikes placed all around the park attractions (i.e. ponds, flower gardens, etc.), cafes, and restaurants, and are easily adjustable for your height preferences. If you don't know a thing about bikes just ask someone around you. The main thing is to adjust the seat, which is fairly easy if you know a thing or two about bikes, but completely understandable if you don't. Ask.

Aside from just the park, the surrounding area is extremely beautiful as well. I think the local town committee incentivize people to decorate their houses to be as aesthetically pleasing and Van Gough-ie as possible, including easels with Van Gough paintings on them, sunflowers, and other little cutesy things.

AND. If you're really nuts for the guy, head down to Nuenen, where he was born (also where my dietician lives.) I know of one guy on AirBnb who specializes in giving Van Gough tours of the area, as well as a tour group that does multi-day bike tours of the area, both of which you can find with a quick Google search. And if you're looking to lose weight I can give you my dietician's number. There are also some cool cities in the vicinity for you to check out.

30. Head South for Carnival

Happen to be visiting around February-March? Decided you DID want to feed your Van Gough obsession and see Nuenen? Or was it my dietician that you're really after? You're in luck, my friend. Although the date changes every year, typically in the last or second to last weekend of February Carnival begins in the south. While Amsterdam has King's Day, Brabant and Limburg have Carnival. Stemming from Catholic origins, Carnival is most glamorously celebrated in Limburg, the southern most province of the Netherlands kissing Belgium and Germany, but is still enjoyable in Brabant as well. Every town is given a silly name in Olde Dutch. The kick-off of this three day extravaganza begins with the mayor symbolically handing over the keys of the city to the Prince of Carnival who, with his band of merrymakers, will begin parading the streets and gracing the pubs of their area with cheers of "Alaaf!"

My recommendation would be to check out Maastricht, a major city in Limburg where they'll still be English speakers aplenty (Limburg has its own dialect and not everyone is guaranteed to speak English as they are in the North.) The streets are figuratively flooded with bouts of celebration, over-the-top costumes, music, laughter, merriment, and, of course beer.

"Some tourists think Amsterdam is a city of sin, but in truth it is a city of freedom. And in freedom, most people find sin."

— John Green, The Fault in Our Stars

31. Live Local

A majority of Amsterdamians don't actually live in Amsterdam. To many, Amsterdam is more for the tourists and the students, enjoyed occasionally on for nights out or festivals but better to relax and chill without the background noise of "I didn't know they were just, like, in windows like that, y'know?"

For a cheaper room and a real experience getting to know the kind of people who run Amsterdam, check out my city: Utrecht. Utrecht is to Amsterdam what Brooklyn is to Manhattan. While the glitz and glam of the big cities are alluring to tourists, the real grit is better found in these outlaying areas. In a 30 minute train ride you'll run into what many see as the more trendy city of the Netherlands. You'll hear this argument from many people in defense of many other cities (usually based on locality) but Utrecht really is where it's at. From vegan restaurants to underground clubs, you won't fall short of things to do in Utrecht.

More suited for a day trip, my tip is to walk along Wittevrouwensingel which outlines the meat of the city, stop for lunch at Biltstraat, Pickles being one of the family favorites but there are many more, spend some time exploring, and head to the Oudegracht for a nice diner along the canal, Pannenkoekenbakkerij (Pancake bakery) De Muntgelder being my personal go-to when visitors come, and wrap up with some drinks at one of the many taverns at Neude.

32. Visit The Hague

Rich in history and things to do, Den Haag (The Hague) plays an important role in the Netherlands. The Netherlands is a kingdom with a royal family still in tact, with its own Government System, Parliament, Supreme Court, and Council of State, all of which can be found in Den Haag. The Royal Palace is found in Dam Square and is normally open to visitors with the exception of any royal events, King Willem-Alexander more frequently residing in Den Haag in The Noordeinde Palace and Villa Eikenhorst in Wassenaar. Aside from visiting governmental and historical buildings in Den Haag, there are frequent events, festivals, a plethora of museums, gardens, and a beach in the area. It goes without saying that there are, of course, a variety of eating and drinking options, as well as nightlife to go around.

33. Love Your Children

Part of Dutch culture is the important role children play in society, as well as the role of their parents, which is not to strictly monitor everything their children do, but rather to encourage their children to become smart, independent, autonomous beings capable of living happy and full lives. You see this pattern repeating a lot in the way that society functions and people interact. As a brief example, I've been told that this value for children has a lot to do with the bike culture, as children can be safer and more independent with fewer cars and more bike lanes than they would be should the situation be reversed. Many other expats I've spoken with are baffled by the amazing independence of young Dutch children, but in a way it feels like the whole society is prepared for this concept. Nonetheless, as a result of this, the Dutch have some pretty amazing kid stuff that will make your inner child rile with envy.

34. Interact with NEMO

NEMO is an interactive science museum "for children of all ages." When they say "of all ages" they really mean "for children and it's not so bad for their guardians." On my first trip to Amsterdam my friend decided it would be GREAT if I came here, completely skipping all of the other fun touristy things that you want to do on your first trip to a city. It is a very impressive museum and, in typical Dutch style, they have phenomenal fun stuff for the kids to play with and on. Trampolines, jungle gyms, ball pits, interactive CGI animations, and so much more that you need to see to believe. All of which with science-y spin, so kids can have fun while learning some interesting stuff. Everything is accessible in both English and Dutch. Not to mention they have lockers that you can keep your stuff in, baby changing areas, wheelchair accessibility (including bathrooms), exhibits accessible for visually impaired, and, of course, First Aid. Safety first.

35. Check Out That Zoo!

As you may have noticed, the Netherlands is a kingship, and so the zoo is, naturally, a Royal Zoo. Natural Artis Magistra, or Artis Royal Zoo, is located right near Waterlooplein and Wertheimpark and is the oldest zoo in the Netherlands as well as one of the oldest zoos in Europe. It boasts a whopping 900 species and also hosts an aquarium and a planetarium as well.

Naturally, there are cafes and toilets around the zoo, so you never have to leave! They offer a variety of educational programs and events offered throughout the day, not to mention special events that come up at different times throughout the year, such as the upcoming Gay Pride event during the time of the Gay Pride Festival. And, at an extra cost, you can visit Micropia, the microbe exhibition.

This zoo is for everyone. The terrain is mostly wheelchair accessible, with handicapped parking subject to normal requirements and wheelchairs available to rent for the day at €1.00. It is not, however, welcome to other animals including service animals, unfortunately. They are welcome in Micropia and Artis Square

36. Experience Dutch Kiddie Culture

Children's amusement parks in the Netherlands are nothing short of spectacular. For the real gems, however, you need to leave Amsterdam. Trust me: it's worth it. There is nothing in this world that can compare to Efteling. This is *actually* fun for the whole family. Try to avoid coming in the summer time if you can, as some lines can be excruciating, especially if you plan on staying in Amsterdam and want to make a full day of this adventure.

Come when it opens to experience the most spectacular water show you've ever seen in your entire life and then come back again at the closing show to see the NEW most spectacular water show you've ever seen in your entire life.They have water shows periodically throughout the day but the opening and closing ones are by far the most astonishing ones. Be prepared to say "WOW!"

Continue on to the Fairy Tale Forest where you and your kids can enjoy automated reenactments of your favorite fairy tales, spoken in Dutch with descriptions in English, French, Dutch, and German. Take the train around the park to catch the major attractions. You don't want to miss Ravelijn (the dragon show), Droomvlucht, or the Gondola. Dutch amusement parks really go all out for the theme, these attractions are the stuff of ride engineers' dreams. If you're in it for the thrills, they've got plenty of roller coasters, De Vliegende Hollander (Flying Dutchman), Vogel Rok (Eagle Rock), and Joris en de Draak (Joris and the Dragon) are my recommendations. Fanta Morgana, Carnaval Festival, and Droomvlucht are three of their must-see "Dark Rides" that leave you feeling things.

If you're feeling peckish check out one of their many cafés, restaurants, pancake houses, or sweet shops. My recommendation is Pinokkio's Restaurant for a nice variety and some time to sit down.

37. Spend the Day at Slagharen

Slagharen Themepark and Resort is home to a number of different family friendly activities. Appropriately named Vakantiepark (vacation park) Slagharen is home to 30 different shows and attractions, not to mention the waterpark and the resort, which includes bike rentals, super market, laundromat, swimming pool, animal park, and everything else you need to have a luxury family adventure. Just want a day trip? They've got you covered with lockers and amenities, of course. The parks are made to be wheelchair friendly, animal friendly, and the cafes are even able to accommodate dietary and allergen restrictions. Wow.

38. Dive with the Dolphins

If after this your kids are still left unamused, check out the Dolfinarium in Hardewijk. Again, the Dutch go all out with the theme. Begin with Aqua Bella dolphin show that transcends time and space. You can take time after the show to meet and greet with the dolphins at an additional cost. Continue with De Snor(rrr)show (walrus show), and the Adventure Island sea lion show. They have a number of other shows and attractions that are updated regularly and, as one would expect, multiple different exhibits where you can view and interact with animals in the dolphinarium just as you would in a regular aquarium.

And, not to worry, they have of course a dining hall and multiple snack and gift shops scattered throughout the park. Don't be daunted by the parking lot. Just follow the crowds to the busses that take you directly to the main entrance, just don't forget where you parked!

39. Cuddle with Cats

If you're, like me, a cat person frequently missing your favorite feline at home, you'll find many spots around Amsterdam where you can get your furry fix. While a variety of pubs and cafes have their own resident cats, first and foremost is the semi-famous cat cafe Kopjes Cat Café in Oud-West. Here you can enjoy a purrfect breakfast, lunch, or drink of choice alongside some new female friends. Though, as a cat person, my consistent problem with cat cafes is the "you can look but you can't touch" attitude of the cats. But I guess they're over all these people trying to get their attention.

The Kattenkabinet (Cat Cabinet) is a cat museum in Amsterdam Centraal that features a variety of cat and cat-themed artwork, not to mention the resident cats who often peak their little faces around the museum.

Pozenboot (Paws boat or S.S. Paws, as I like to call it) is houseboat-turned-cat-sanctuary where abandoned, abused, or stray cats are rescued, rehabilitated, and given shelter. If you want to get your kitty cuddles in while you're perusing the canals, stop here for a quick fix, just be sure to check their website for their hours of operation, as they vary a bit.

40. Stroll Through Jordaan

Jordaan is an area of Amsterdam West thats filled with all sorts of pleasant shops, restaurants, snack spots, and cafés. Be sure to walk up Tuinstraat and Tlweedetuindwarstraat in search of some very refreshing shops sporting second hand, quirky, and locally made goods. Head up Prinsengracht towards the Noorderkerk (Northern Church), where they have the Boerenmarkt (Farmer's Market) on Saturday and the Noordermarkt (Northern Market) on Monday and Saturday. Scan the city for all sorts of lovely restaurants, cafes, shops, galleries, and independent movie theaters. See my recommendations in the next chapters.

"People, houses, streets, animals, flowers-everything in Holland looks as if it were washed and ironed each night in order to glisten immaculately and newly starched the next morning."

Felix Marti-Ibanez

41. Eat your Vegetables

My boyfriend refers to Jordaan as the "hipster" area of town, and admittedly it is pretty gentrified. After five years as a vegan, however, I've come to learn that hipster areas are vegan paradise, home to the over-the-top, cozy-cuddly, served-on-a-board-in-a-mason-jar type restaurants and cafés that offer food that we actualy can eat *and* tastes good! Yes, it's probably over priced but it's a price that we're willing to pay, especially considering what we save thanks to all of the other places with no veg*n options. Of these hipster veg*n places, Bolhoed on Prinsengracht is on the top of the list of noteworthiness. It's a vegetarian restaurant with a lot of vegan options, including vegan pastry options, so you can have your cake and eat it too!

42. Try Some Chocolate

Hankering for something sweet? If you are a choc-o-haulic you're going to want to go to Sweet Bob Amsterdam on Brouwersgracht. This gourmet pastry shop sells a variety of truffles and bonbons that are sure to make your mouth water just in passing. Stop here to cure your sweet tooth, take some home for that chocolate lover at home. My friends and family from the States are always shocked at the quality of chocolate in the Netherlands, but really this should come as no surprise if you think about the proximity of their Dutch-speaking, chocolate-loving neighbors, Belgium. Treat thy self!

43. Eat the Best Dutch Apple Pie in Town!

I promise I'm not just leading your down a canal of questionable life decisions, now you see why I needed that dietician in Nuenen. Also located on the Noordermarkt, Winkel 43 (Shop 43) is locally known as the best apple pie in town. With a lovely ambiance and a variety of other non-apple pie options, if you're looking to try some real and renowned Dutch Apple Pie look no further!

44. Sing-A-Long

Jordaan is well known for its bubbling atmosphere. Check out different bars that offer karaoke, sing-a-long, and other lively song-and-dancy activities. Bars such as Café Nol (Altijd Lol : Always Fun) are good to visit for some sing-a-long fun. Come in September to enjoy Jordaan Festival where you can listen to live Dutch folk music and classics.

45. Stop for a Drink

While in Jordaan you will have plenty of tempting drink options. Check out Finch Café on the Noordermarkt. This café is scenically located just off the canal and is always filled with laughter and good conversation. Stop in for some eats and drinks in the style of that one friend of yours who knows how to cook. Not feeling it? There are so many bars in this area you're bound to run into one on the way to the next suggestion: Café Thijssen. This is a pretty standard bar, snacks, beers, canals. What more could you ask for?

46. Grab-And-Go!

A bit further north-west of Jordaan you'll run into Haarlemmerbuurt, most specifically Haarlemmerstraat, Haarlemmerdijk, and Haarlemmerplein. This somewhat more commercial area is host to a multitude of bubbling bars and restaurants to choose from. In this area you can find your Dutch goodies staples: Stash, Coffeecompany, and Marqt. These are all good options for keeping it real when you're on-the-go. Try the filter coffee at Coffeecompany, or a latte if that's your preference. Stop at Stash or Marqt for some delicious and nutritious on-the-go food options and enjoy it in nearby Westerpark. Feed your sweet-tooth *again* with *one of* Stash's delectable sweet treats. Also check out DIS in Haarlemmerplein. I haven't been, due to my severe loyalty to Stash, but rumor has it DIS is delish.

47. Unwind in Westerpark

After picking up all of those goodies in Harlemmersbuurt, head over to Westerpark for some down time. Bring your own blanket or park-up on one of their benches or (slightly sketchy looking) picnic tables. Relax by the pond or wander around to find a spot that meets your heart's desire. There's a playground for the kids to play on and plenty of room for some soccer/football, frisbee, or other fun field game-playing. Furry friends are welcome and public toilets are also available. On the other side of the park you'll run into the lovely Tuinpark (Garden park) Nut & Genoegen as as well as Volkstuinvereniging (People's Garden Association) Sloterdijkermeer, a scenic view for your walkabout.

48. Check out Westergasfabriek

Smack in the middle of Westerpark is the Westergasfabriek. You'll notice here a bunch of different buildings. Some of them are business buildings, educational buildings, restaurants, cafés, and shops. Take time to browse around and see what feels nice to you. Stop in Het Ketelhuis (The Kettle House), a former factory building now acting as an arthouse movie theater. The theater also hosts a café and restaurant. It's also possible to buy one of their "Film & Diner" packages. Films change frequently so check out their website for more info.

Just across the way is Zuiveringshal West, home to markets, events, expos, and exhibits, as well as Gashouder, used for Amsterdam Fashion Week and other events, Transformation Huis, used for conferences and lounge events, Westergastheater, the theater, Machinegebouw, used for presentations and dinners, Leidingshuis, The Main House available for rent similar to an AirBnb, and the Werkkamer, office space for daily rent. Around this area you'll find many public open air events, such as music festivals and fun fairs.

49. Plan for Festival Season

If you're like me, than the word "festival" usually refers to some three day camping event in which a lot of drugs and/or questionable activity occurs while live music is played non-stop throughout the day. Dutch festivals are a little different. First of all, they're public. Sometimes they'll have a cover charge of €10-20 but it's not often that a festival will be sold out or that you can't buy tickets at the door. To compare it to what I'm used to as an American, they're basically like gigantic street fairs, open air events, concert series, or carnivals.

You'll have a few stages for music and dancing, you almost always need to buy these ridiculous tokens that are specific to that festival which you can only use to buy food and drinks, and there's usually something offered for the kids, or at the very least there will be kids present. And yes, people may be on drugs but it's much more casual (erratic behavior at the minimum) compared to what I've seen at festivals in the U.S. There are so many of them that it would be ridiculous to list them all, but a few notable ones are: King's Day, Liberation Day, Dance Valley, Amsterdam Music Festival and, outside of Amsterdam, GLOW (Eindhoven) and Carnival which are both in Brabant.

50. Party Like a King

King's Day is probably the biggest festival in the Netherlands, mostly because they celebrate it in Amsterdam, whereas Carnival is strictly for the south. The date changes every year but it's usually in the springtime. Everything begins the night before on King's Evening, as it's called, which is know to be best celebrated in Utrecht and King's Day itself in Amsterdam. King's Day is the kickoff of festival season, the whole city is alight with parties and music. The best thing is that all of it is free! You can party on a boat and cruise the canals or walk the city from DJ booth to DJ booth, like a city-wide block party. The dress code is everything and anything ORANGE!

> TOURIST
Greater than a Tourist

Please read other Greater than a Tourist Books.

Join the >Tourist Mailing List :
http://eepurl.com/cxspyf

Facebook:
https://www.facebook.com/GreaterThanATourist

Pinterest:
http://pinterest.com/GreaterThanATourist

Instagram:
http://Instagram.com/GreaterThanATourist

Please leave your honest review of this book on Amazon and Goodreads. Thank you

Printed in Great Britain
by Amazon

21215788R00051